The Taste of Flesh

Dennis Hathaway

The Taste of Flesh

Copyright © 2018 by Dennis Hathaway

All rights reserved. No part of this book may be reproduced or transmitted in any form or by any means without written permission of the author.

ISBN 978-1-7324762-0-2

Published by:

Crania Press
1072 Palms Blvd.
Venice, CA 90291

Contents

The Promised Land 1
Santa Inez 3
Memory 5
Sway 7
Christmas Day, 2001 9
Cream 12
Father 16
Money 20
Queen Of Spades 24
The Invention Of Ideas 26
The Taste Of Flesh 29
Elegy For Larry 32
Desire 34
The Philosophy Of Love 36
The Path 37
River Of Wind 40
Fauna 42
Southern California (Revised) 44
The Harrying Of The North 46
Documents Of War 48
For Laura, On Valentine's Day 50
For Laura, On Her Birthday 53
For Gabrielle 55
Forever 57
Coda 59

THE PROMISED LAND

Route 66 somewhere south of our childhood,
Unseen but not unconsidered.
Part of the plan to escape
The tragedy of nothingness.

But nothing begets nothing
And substance overrules style
So that sliding along the highway at eighty,
Bluster of wind on the arm cocked
Through the open window,
The cracked lanes spooling away in the rear-view mirror,
The Tareyton smoldering on the arch of the steering wheel,
The smirk on the driver's face

Mean nothing.
Life is destination.
The stucco and palm tree infinity of Los Angeles
Tingling through the viscera like an erotic dream
Unseen but not unfelt, a virus of uncertain consequence.

We will blunder, somewhere in the gray desert,
Lose our trail, like pioneers destined to starve
Unless willing to eat our own kind.

Dennis Hathaway

We will find ourselves in Bakersfield,
A tragedy of a lesser order.

A hot wind howls from the mountain
Bringing news of war, famine, pestilence.
Cars boil on the side of the grade,
But none of it really matters, or can be clearly heard
Above the insistence of forward motion,
The hum and rattle of a great idea.

SANTA INEZ

We'll drink the wine
We bought that summer day.
The hills outside the winery yellow,
The sun warm but distant
Like a vanished lover's embrace.

And I'll remember the flutter of candles
On angel food cake,
And stiff white combers of frosting,
And I'll hear my father sing my name
And see him smile,
For the first time in weeks,
Months, perhaps even years.

Like amateurs we gulped the wine
While others sniffed, swirled, spat.
We couldn't taste the difference
Between the special estate deluxe reserve
And the $4.99 bottle snatched off
The supermarket shelf because
We liked the label.

And I'll remember drinking blackberry brandy
In the back seat of a '59 Ford
With my arm around a girl whose lips were answers
To secrets so forbidden that just for a moment
I was deathly afraid.

The pleasant middle-aged woman pouring
Said, *Would you like to try this?*
And in our eager unsophisticated way we
Said, *That's really good*, and
We asked the price and she said
Sixty dollars and we stared at each other
And then we said *Why not?*
Even though we'd never paid more than
Ten for a bottle of wine before.

And my father said blow out the candles,
And I tried, I tried, but one flickered,
Like the tongue of a snake
In a dream, deadly, terrifying,
And my tears turned everything into
A broken, shattered vision
Of what might come.

MEMORY

What did I do yesterday, between the hours of nine and twelve,
And why does it matter, parsing the memory,
When the big truths—that water boils at 212 degrees Fahrenheit,
    for example—resist the fatality of time. Is it winter now?

Or do the splitting seams of earth emit the rapture of life
In ways resistant to the logic of the patriarchs, which is to say,
What we know of seeds and other particles is impermanent,
Will fade, oxidize, retract to an infant's temperamental myopia.

They got it wrong, the ones who said *knowledge is power*.
Knowledge is the infant's state of helpless need and fury.
    Knowledge kills.
I was somewhere, at some moment, doing something.
And summer's plague is neither heat, nor mosquitoes,
Nor the dissonant jangle of the ice cream truck.
Summer's plague is the knowledge that a green leaf will
    brown and wither,
And who will care? Who will perform a rite? Deliver a eulogy?
I don't know anyone who has the time.

What did I read in the newspaper this morning. Did it have
    to do with the Mideast?

An easy guess, hardly any effort required.
But the words themselves present a certain difficulty.
For example: Once I was sitting in the Lafayette Café on Venice Beach eating huevos rancheros when a man reading a magazine at the next booth asked the meaning of *peripatetic* and I was the only one in the immediate vicinity to rattle off the definition.
At the time I was trying to get on Jeopardy!

Peripatetic. I could look it up, I suppose, but that requires more effort than seems necessary.
Who was Tamerlane? How many inches in a meter? What is a *bildungsroman*, for God's sake?!
We could all look it up, together, if we could remember where we put the dictionary.

SWAY

A body of water, deep, azure, pure.
A boat, sleek, sail full of wind,
Tacking into sunlight so brilliant
That love and hate are nothing more than words
Whispered beneath the slap and whip and crash
Of forward progress.

The man, a neophyte, abandons the sway of the deck
For the chop of the lake named after a Native American
Once known to be an Indian
Once known to be a powerful, crafty chief
Brought down by gunpowder, superior numbers, and
Last but hardly least, the Christian faith.

Which says: Skepticism is the devil's angle,
The seeing in the layers of water an infinite variety
Of Things. The suspicion that every answer
Poses a question, that facts are tumbleweeds,
Rolling across an arid landscape in front of a
Relentless wind.

The man's wife, a good swimmer, jumps in after him.
Why? To save him? The picture is blurred by the

Absence of Omniscience, the motion that renders
Every moment infinitely brief, a blink of the eye
Like unto an hour, a day, a lifetime.

An observer might say, *She tried to save him.*
A second might say, *It was sort of hard to tell
What was going on.*
A bad novelist might explain, directly, or with
Clumsy devices; the police will theorize, the
Men and women of the village beyond the dock
Will gossip, the children will remember only
In their dreams.

But witnesses who believe they saw the wife
Push her husband down
As he struggled against the lure of the deep,
As he conceded the inevitability of the moment
Are mistaken.

Or if not mistaken, literally, then deluded
For delusion is the engine
That drives such matters.
And thus I am here to testify that I love my wife
Who is a good swimmer
Who has shown her love for me in many ways
Impossible to falsify, and that I
Am here, and alive, and well.

CHRISTMAS DAY, 2001

Reading Billy Collins in Twenty-Nine Palms
And the story of Fillipo Brunelleschi who
Raised the great cathedral dome in Florence,
City of tourists milling shopping gazing circling
Michaelangelo's David with his oversized hands
And smooth marble genitalia unlikely to frighten anyone,
Not even children.

Beyond the thin connecting door a TV
Blathers, and the coyote with sharp pointed ears
Stands in the middle of the road with nothing to fear
From trucks and automobiles, which, after all,
Are nothing but the waking vestiges
Of mad scientists' dreams.

He (or she) will join the midnight chorus yipping *Silent Night,*
But we are deaf,
Reading Billy Collins who deftly turns a phrase
Like a chef flipping pancakes, or a casino dealer shuffling cards.
Reading of Fillipo's invention of a hoist
In the city of Davids, some tall and buff, others
Slender, like Donatello's naked boy, some miniature,
Carved in wood long since turned to dust.

We trudge into the sharp wind, sun climbing in
And out of its bed of cloud.
In the shelter of a rock we eat muffins saved
From the continental breakfast—the term a fuse
That sputters through the streets of Paris, from a forgotten
Rue near the *Jardin de Luxembourg* past the cafes and
Patisseries and fromageries over the Pont du something or other
To the Louvre, where the Mona Lisa sadly huddles in her box
    of bulletproof glass.
Tourists straining gawking at the world's most famous woman,
More famous than Julia Roberts, more famous than the Queen.

In the U.S. a lawyer would have filed a Writ of Habeas Corpus
On her behalf.

But this is France, with its Gallic eccentricities, and Italy,
Where a train conductor insists that your ticket to Venice
Is lacking a supplement.
A woman who looks nothing like *La Gioconda*.
A blonde thirty-something woman imprisoned in her uniform
And bureaucratic tenacity,
Who gives up with a churlish toss of her hands.
Hopeless middle-aged American who speaks Italian with
All the aptitude
Of a dog driving a car

Far from Twenty-Nine Palms, home of the Marine Haircut,
Shops that alter uniforms, motels with tumbleweeds
Rolling up to the doors.

In the silent morning, the neighbor's TV euthanized,
Billy Collins devising an image, Fillipo Brunelleschi

The Taste of Flesh

Inventing yet another hoist, Parisians sunning themselves
Beside the Seine,
The desert air ruffles the fan palm outside the window
And we lie face to face, bosom to chest, preparing
In the unhurried calm of the holiday
To make love.

CREAM

He crosses the frozen earth
Between the barn and milk house,
A huff of steam in front of his face,
Buckets at the ends of his arms
Swinging slightly, the contents
Sloshing gently against the sides—
Mild white surf.

Inside, the separator stands prepared,
Stainless steel funnel above
The conical centrifuge, the twin spouts.
Its inventor reasoning from ancient observation
That cream, given time, will rise,
And allow itself to be skimmed.

He upends one bucket,
Turns the crank,
Whistles a tune
That cannot be identified
Above the whine of the centrifuge,
The rattle of the loose tin roof
In the punishing wind.

The Taste of Flesh

When the poles that march across the valley
Are draped with wires,
And the kerosene lamps are put away,
And a radio is plugged into the wall,
The separator will come to life
With the toggle of a switch.

No more cranking.
The horses have already disappeared,
So suddenly as to be a trick.
Their discourse of snorts and whinnies,
Displaced by the prosody of a two-cylinder John Deere—
Johnny-popper in the farmer's lingo.

The only thing you can predict, he says,
With a note of regret in his voice,
As if offended by a lover's inconstancy,
Is that everything will change.

The frozen earth will thaw,
The drifts of snow will shrink,
Leaking rivers of pure water.
The separator will rust, unused,
Discarded like an item of worn, out-of-fashion clothing,
And his head will turn gray, then white,
And he will speak in a voice not quite nostalgic,
And not quite tarnished with bitterness.

He will remember the snow drifted against the barn,
He will remember the horses that bolted, or kicked, or
    otherwise misbehaved,
Like surly children;

He will remember those children, and his wife, and his
    own father,
Dispensing wisdom that went down like medicine,
And he will feel that straggling line of ancestry,
Disappearing into the past.

And then he will sigh, and all will be quiet, and gone.

The Taste of Flesh

FATHER

Your silence in repose,
Your closed eyes,
Your sealed lips

That yield no answer to the question:
Why? Why do father and son
Find themselves in the cold winter of strife,
When the season calls for friendship and camaraderie,
For the summer warmth of deep affection
Collected in the basement of shared history.

Who were you?

A phenomenon of strength
Who could pull trees from the ground by the roots,
Who could lift houses from their foundations,
Who could walk for months across the rugged earth
Without a moment of rest or faltering.

You knew the answers to all questions:
How many square feet in an acre,
What a change in wind direction portends,
Why a dog turns a circle before lying down.

The Taste of Flesh

Afflicted with doubt and uncertainty
The son clumps around the bedroom in your ship-like shoes,
And wonders how his miniature appendages
Will ever grow to such impressive size.

Appalled by darkness and unseen things,
The son quavers while you calmly consider
The flashes of lightning in the black night,
The abyss at the edge of the creek,
The bloated cow with hooves pointing to the sky.

You were ill, once, maybe twice.
And the sight of you, supine,
Was disorienting. Like the windmill steadily whirring
Day upon day, then one morning
Still, horizontal, as silent as the ominous night.

You were the oak tree in the hollow.
You were the yellow bluff behind the barn.
You were the stream of water in the creek.
You were the wind that blew across the ridge.
You were constant, unmoving, unmovable,
And as the son shakes off the burden of expectation,
Causing, in his egocentric thoughtlessness,
Pain as sharp as any that might be felt
With a careless blow of the hammer,
Fear as intense as any you might feel,
With the sudden shift of the earth beneath your feet.

And the words lay stiffly on the son's tongue:
I'm sorry. They won't emerge from history's
Muffled catacombs. I love you. The words

Circle inside the head like a hawk that has
Spotted a mouse in the long grass of a field.

Will you listen? Will you hear the words,
If they can be formed, written, laid upon the page?

You have no means to nod,
You have no way to smile a wry smile,
To say something humorous.
You cannot lift your strong hand.
You cannot say the word, *Son*.

The shoes still don't fit, although they'd do in an emergency.
The thrashing against rules, proscriptions, aphoristic advice,
These unruly facts are part of a past containing
Tail fins, spinner hub caps, Ed Sullivan on TV.

Facts trivial but of enormous consequence,
Because they furnished two lives,
Lives often distant, but never broken
Into parts that floated into separate universes.

Father and son,
The conjunction the most common in the language.
Without the son the father does not exist.
And vice-versa. The bond cannot be broken.
Not even by the most violent splitting of atoms.

And thus the son says, *Goodbye*.
Your strength, your endurance, your aphorisms,
They will settle with you into the earth
Which goes on, which persists despite our wanton recklessness,

And into the dust will settle anger, resentment, guilt, sorrow,
And you will be remembered,
And loved.

MONEY

Good Evening, Ladies and Gentlemen. As chairman of the Finance Committee, I have been asked to deliver some remarks on the subject of money. This is a subject with which I have some acquaintance. One morning, not long ago, I awoke to discover that I had none. Money, I'm speaking of. My wallet was as empty as a politician's promise. My penny jar did not contain a single coin. My ATM card wouldn't work because my account balance had fallen <u>below</u> zero.

I was broke
I was broken
I was chokin' on the bone of no success
The bone of contention, retention, detention
Intention
Intention is the root of all evil
Who said that?
Bush. George B. George be nimble, George be quick, George
    jump over the candle—Wait a minute
Wait an hour
Wait a day
A day for pay and finally, finally, a roll in the hay
You say, they say, we say, naysay
Nattering nabobs of negativism—we will have our day.

The Taste of Flesh

I went to the credit union
to make a balloon payment
A ballooning payment.
Pay, say, lay, gray, hay
Gray hay feeds no livestock
No lively stock
No lively hood

The liveliest hood is right here
We got banks and cranks and shanks and someday
We might even have tanks
Tanks of money. Tanks of love. Tanks for which we give thanks
Thanks for giving. Thanks for getting. Thanks for going.
Thanks for being all you can be and even a little more
A little more might make you sore,
Might lead to war
Might feed the poor
If they would only recognize
The severity of their condition
Their condition, their conditioning, their air conditioning
On the blink, never installed, never even dreamed about
They got fans, pans, cans, LANS
Networks
Nets <u>do</u> work. Just ask the fish.

But they can't talk, not in English
The tongue of our fathers, our brothers, our mothers,
    our druthers
Speak it. Seek it. Leak it. Let it all hang out.
Let it all hang in. Out. In. Down. Up. Over. Under,
    plunder, sunder
All into halves, have-nots, forget-me-nots, roses.

Flowers for the poor, the whore, the core of true believers.
I prayed for money
I listened for an answer
I waited, I prated, I collated, I wasted paper.

What does it have to do with money? Money is funny just ask the accountant.
Money is honey just ask the beekeeper.
Money is runny just watch it go through your fingers.

You must save. Open an account with a man in a suit who may be a brute to boot but that is moot in light of the fact that you are forced to root for the losing team. The failures, the losers, the cruisers, the Chevy Impalas, the Fords, the Nixons, the presidents all making fools of themselves. Fools of us. Fools of the United Nations.
Fools, tools, renewals, accruals, money.

You didn't think we'd close that circle, did you?

The Taste of Flesh

QUEEN OF SPADES

I wouldn't wish my life on anyone.
I love parties.
I love to dress up.
But black? Always black?
Never red? Yellow? Turqoise?

Nobody wants to see me.
Nobody.
Not that weird little guy
Who's always the first to arrive.
With those stubby arms
And little round head
He looks like a freeway intersection.
He's always in black, too.
Doesn't he have any imagination?

And that bunch that always dresses in red.
Who are they?
Once or twice they were all together,
They gathered around me,
They made me feel special.
The hosts, too.
They brought me drinks, little sandwiches,

Chocolate-covered strawberries.
They treated me like a person,
Not a disease.

But these little red people—
They're some kind of tribe or clan,
They've got a king and queen, for god's sake.
They're usually scattered around,
They usually look right through me
Like I'm invisible.

When the others see me
They pretend to look away,
Or they cringe.

I'd cry if I thought
It would make me feel better.

THE INVENTION OF IDEAS

It would be interesting (for someone)
To examine the persistence of failed ideas.

Propositions that don't bear scrutiny.
For example: The trickle-down theory.

Why not the trickle-up theory? Money in
The hands of the poor will find its way to the rich

Who own the banks, the fast-food franchises,
The automobile dealerships.

A museum of failed ideas:
The square wheel, the faceless clock, Christianity.

For aren't ideas really gasps of confusion?
Smeared ink? Blackboards imperfectly erased?

For example: The trickle-down theory,
A nice turn of phrase, almost poetic

And more revealing than perhaps it was meant to be
By its inventor, Mr. so-and-so with such-and-such degree.

The Taste of Flesh

Trickle, verb, *To flow or fall in drops or in a thin stream.*
The idea: A thin stream of money flowing into the middle class

And drops falling through a crack onto the busboy,
The waitress, the taxi driver, the janitor, the gas station attendant

Who attends not to the customer fumbling at the pumps,
But to the cigarettes and candy bars and quarts of 30 weight oil

That furnish his bulletproof cubicle—Another idea: self-service.
Service, noun, *The occupation or duties of a servant.*

Self, noun, *One's own interest, welfare, or advantage.*
You put that together. You do the math.

Dennis Hathaway

THE TASTE OF FLESH

I'm reading an account of the *Essex,*
The ship sunk by a malicious whale,
The captain and crew in boats,
Eating one another to survive.

And I think about sirloin steak
And roasted chicken, and wonder:
How does it taste?
The arm, the hip, the liver, the heart.

The captain first cut off the head,
The hands and the feet,
Threw these items overboard,
So that he could more easily imagine
That he was butchering an animal.

Buried in the snow of Donner Pass
The emigrants ate their cows,
Their horses,
Bark stripped from trees,
Their boots and laces,
Finally themselves.

When I was nineteen I had no money,
No home, no car, no prospects.
Walking head down through the streets,
Watching for lost money
In the litter along the curb.

In the fluorescent gleam of the all-night Laundromat
I tried to sleep on a row of plastic chairs,
Gave up and found a cigarette butt,
Long enough for two or three puffs.
But there were no matches,
No one to give me a light.

I walked the empty streets
To the apartment of a man who had wanted
To get me into his bed.
I knocked on his door
And gruff with sleep his voice delivered the news
That another man was there.
But he gave me a blanket and use of the sofa
Just for the remnant of the night.

I quaked with hunger
Under the thin blanket
And in the fuzz of dawn
Crept through the kitchen opening doors and drawers.

Nothing. No bread, no peanut butter, no sliced bologna, no
    beer or milk or wine.
Nothing but a box of matzos.
Strange, tasteless things for a boy
Just months from a Midwestern farm.

The Taste of Flesh

I ate them all,
Then folded the blanket
And softly closed the door.

If not for the matzos
I would have eaten the curtains
Over the kitchen sink.
The woodwork with its scabby
Layers of paint.
The worn linoleum on the floor.
But would I have eaten one of the men?
The one who softly snored,
Unaware that I was creeping toward the bed
With a long, sharp knife?

ELEGY FOR LARRY

The grace of being
Measured in moments,
Some as brief as a whisper,
Some longer, grander, potent
With friendship, with love.

Morning at the 7-Eleven,
Time a whitewater rush and tumble,
Amidst the fumes of coffee and urgency.
A moment beside the rack of barbecue-flavor potato chips:
What's up, I'm reading this book,
I think you'd like it, hey, good to see you.
We'll get together, talk about it.

The morning stretching in its clamor,
Its callow striving,
But tempered, soothed,
With the ointment of intimate courtesy.

Mexico, late night, something humming,
A generator maybe,
Talk of almost everything,
A pause, not for breath, but curiosity:

The Taste of Flesh

What do you think?
What do you think?
A desire, no, a need, no, a way of being.
Curious, wanting to know what's in the
Other's head, the heart, the soul.

Sunday afternoon, outdoors, nothing to do
But be affronted,
By the newspaper's tidings,
By the cruel, the dishonest, the inhumane
And then, in the flicker of a cool breeze,
The subject Emile Zola, and Paul Cezanne,
The topic creativity, and the social consciousness of art,
And the inscrutable bonds of friendship.

Moments without artifice,
Moments trenchant with seeking,
What is this?
Who are we?
What are we doing?
What does it mean?
Moments like the touches of lovers,
Silent, reverent, unseen.

DESIRE

How did we reach this point,
Without falling, without disappearing
From our own stories
Like inconvenient logic.

I saw you from afar, across a room,
I would have had you, then,
If not for propriety,
And reserve.

Had you as the blade of grass
Has the bead of dew,
Had you as the darkness
Has the light, as the earth
Has the sky.

I hoped, foolishly, but not idly,
For desire isn't idle,
Even if unexpressed, it follows the hours,
Like a shimmer of light
Everywhere.

The Taste of Flesh

THE PHILOSOPHY OF LOVE

Leave it behind, the shaggy, shopworn year,
Say *Goodbye* but not *Good Riddance*,
for that would be unkind, ungenerous,
Given the days that wrapped you in a warm embrace,
That spoke to you of magical charms,
That wooed you as if you were a young woman,
Bursting with the first pangs of desire.

Step through the shadows of unknowingness,
Into the year that will unfold like the pages of a pop-up book,
Sudden eruptions of trees, buildings, people,
Familiar and unknown, but none indifferent to your charms.
Willing, instead, to transport you into the new world,
Where things never imagined are seen, heard, tasted, touched.

I will join you, to share these wonders
Of nature and artifice, the moments that startle,
And delight, and comfort, and quicken, and edify.
I will stand beside you, sit beside you, lie beside you,
And I will wrap you in my arms and speak
Soft nothings to your mind.

THE PATH

Along the way, I saw a rose,
And something about it,
The soft lips of its petals
Just beginning to curl,
To show a tinge of brown.

And the tiny beads of morning dew
Guarding the recesses below,
With their dark mysterious allure,

Made me stop and bend,
And take a long, slow breath
As if I feared the essence hidden there,
As if that breath
Might change me forever.

And I thought of you,
Your essence, your soul,
In those folds and convolutions,
Imperfect in symmetry, in color,
Yet perfect all the same.

And I bent further,
The petals brushed my lips,
I tasted the fleeting dew,
The fragrance seized my mind
And I shuddered.

Stepping back, I felt the prick
Of a thorn,
And saw on my careless hand,
A tiny bead of blood,
Exactly the color of the rose,

And I thought of you,
And smiled.

The Taste of Flesh

RIVER of WIND

River of Wind
That hisses in the
River of Night
That creeps along the
River of Dusk
That ripples over the
River of Dawn
That hides the
River of Darkness
And follows the
River of Light
Into the
River of Silence
Where rises the
River of Belief
And runs the
River of Opportunity
Beside the
River of Promises
That heaves the
River of Sorrow
That weeps the
River of Knowledge

That laughs the
River of Ignorance
Across the
River Side
Within the
River Dale
Beyond the
River View

FAUNA

Unseen, unheard, unimagined,
They were here, in this place,
Where we look, listen, imagine.

Look!

A flutter in the stand of grass. A moment,
As brief as a whisper of silence
In the freighted earth, the burdened sky.

Did you see it?

The crown feather, erect like a helmet plume.
What is she doing?
Where is he going?
Where have they gone?

Listen!

A trill, low as a murmur, nearly lost,
A splash, sudden, trailed by silence eerie as death.
Sounds unshaped, unbidden, commas in the noisy language,
Of the civilized earth.

The Taste of Flesh

Imagine!

You are not here.
This place does not belong to you.
You are one of them.
The scat is yours, you break the water's glassy plane, you
    creep, you wait, you hide.
You are gone. You have come back. This place
Is Yours.

SOUTHERN CALIFORNIA (REVISED)

Spanish bayonet pokes from cracks in the sidewalk
In front of City Hall,
Water trickles around the boulders
In the middle of Pico Boulevard,
Cattle graze outside the Pantry Café,
Soldiers march in the parking lot
Of the 7-Eleven at Palms and Overland.

Creosote bush borders the parched, alkali
Surface of Ventura Boulevard,
A line of cars lurches toward the shimmer
Of an oasis—Van Nuys, Sherman Oaks, Sun Valley,
All mirages thrown up by the relentless sun
That bleaches the bones of those who lingered too long.

They should have listened to the ragged stranger
With the haunted eyes, who pointed north,
To the craggy spine of the Sierra Nevada,
And the fertile green valley to the east.
The gardens and orchards, the soft slap of water in lakes
    and streams,
The happy children playing
In the warm sun and gentle breeze.

THE HARRYING OF THE NORTH

A mother, a child's hand in one of hers,
Her other, palm up, a plea
To one of the men who hold flaming torches
To the roof of her house.

Hic Domus Incenditur
Here a house is burned.

Other men burn crops in the fields,
Barns and sheds and everything
That might fend off the rain and wind and chill
Pouring from the not-so-distant sea.

Everything that might be dropped into a cooking pot,
Roasted, baked, salted, dried, everything
That might relieve the child's
Plaintive cries of hunger

The arsonists giants, the woman and child of ordinary size,
Or perhaps the arsonists of ordinary size and the woman
    and child
Shrunken, diminished, symbols of power
And powerlessness. Impossible to mistake.

The Taste of Flesh

The air shakes with the howl of jets
And the whistle of lethal cargo,
And the woman with the child picks her way
Through shards of glass and wood and stone

And the blood of her husband and sister and grandmother
And aunt and her next door neighbor and the
Keeper of the corner shop and the infant in its
Ruined cradle.

Hic Domus Incenditur
What did the needleworkers feel?
Their hands, the yarn, the linen,
Witnesses to cruelty beyond imagining.

What do we feel? Tourists from a place
Where the houses have roofs,
Where the rivers flow with water
Instead of blood.

We admire the design, the colors, the workmanship,
And we sit in flickering light in our entertainment rooms
And gaze at ruins created not a millennium past
But hours ago.

We gaze at the child in its mother's arms
Gaunt, listless, hot with fever.
In moments it will be wrapped in cloth
And placed into the ground.

Hic Domus Incenditur

DOCUMENTS OF WAR

A letter from a soldier:
Dear Mom and Dad, or *My Darling Wife*; *My Dearest Husband*.
Choose a name—Natalie, Mike, Sarah, any will do.
Miss you, Hope to see you soon, Love to all.
Imagine boxes of letters, in dusty bottoms of drawers.
Imagine the ragged flaps of envelopes
Torn by the implements of haste,
And a photograph of that soldier,
Or another, posing in front of a machine.
Smiling. A machine the color of the dust
From whence he came, to which she shall return.

A letter from a commanding officer:
Dear Mr. and Mrs.—Smith, Garcia, you choose the name.
An official document: Military Letter of Condolence.
Imagine the lieutenant, the captain, the major
Consulting guidelines: *Keep letters sincere and in simple*
language. Show a warm, personal interest in the soldier
and the addressee. Extend condolences and describe the circumstances
surrounding the soldier's death or missing status.

Imagine the places the soldier walked,
Where she sat, ate, where he drove, slept.

Imagine those spaces empty, dry, gray.
Imagine faces broken into shards of grief,
Above a casket littered by a harsh splatter of soil.

Include known facts about the member,
and if appropriate,
include complimentary remarks about:
Character.
Personality.
Achievements.

Facts. Scraps as brittle as the leaves
That scuttle across the grave's disturbed soil
In the chill breath of coming winter,
When the green promise of spring
Is just another falsehood whispered
Across the ravaged earth.

FOR LAURA, ON VALENTINE'S DAY

We could go dancing, sip champagne, stay up late,
We could eat caviar and imported chocolate
At a candlelit table with a red rose in a crystal vase
And a cloud of music wafting above our heads,
Each tipped forward, together, eyes in a kind of embrace,
Hands across the white linen tablecloth, fingers meeting,
Where meaning blooms without the benefit of words.

We could fly around the world in a private jet,
Stopping in Paris, Rome, the other places where
Ardor fills the air like sunlight and fog, and
We could examine the geography of desire,
Like students, excited by the prospect of learning
Those things hidden by layers of words.

We could look into the shimmering distance
And see ourselves, naked, or bundled against the cold,
Walking a path to the highest place on earth,
And we could look out over mountain peaks,
And the roofs of houses, and trees and flowers and grass,
And see everything we've never seen,
Hear everything that's never been put into words.

The Taste of Flesh

We can imagine this as we lie together,
In a familiar bed, our bodies moving
In a slow dance that has no name, our lips
Warm with words so private
They can't be heard.
Words so tender they have no echo,
But live with us, unforgotten, to the end of the world.

Dennis Hathaway

FOR LAURA, ON HER BIRTHDAY

Thinking about nothing, unimportant things,
Then a voice, as familiar as my own,
A face, as expected as the sunrise,
As welcome, saying that we must remember,
And then we must forget:

That day, New York, the first commercial helicopter
Licensed for commercial use.
Things that thrash the air like angry mutant fowl,
Why do we want them?

Your kindness trickles through the rocky
Tangles of another's self-absorption:
Did you know that the House of Commons discussed,
Among other weighty matters, the shortage of stitched
    cotton mops?
The refusal of wholesalers to distribute hot water bottles?

Did you know—you did of course, in some mental realm—
That Harry Truman held a press conference, and discussed,
Among other matters, the settlement of the steelworker's strike?

What does it mean, this long wedge of the past,
Plowing into the mists of the future? That
Noisy gusts of change cannot rattle
The windows we gaze through,
At each other?

We are broad, we are infinite,
We are of the world, its parts—Finland,
Where Juho Kusti Paasivivi began his term
As Prime Minister; Nuremberg, where the
Defense opened its case with evidence that
Goering wasn't the monster he was made out to be,
By the United States, and its vengeful Jews.

And last but hardly least,
J. Edgar Hoover was awarded the Presidential Medal of Merit.

Let us remember and let us forget,
And let us go on together from this eventful date,
With hope, with kindness,
And especially, with love.

FOR GABRIELLE

Great moments heave and rumble
Seize our attention like
A phantasm of special effects
Occupy us
Like an unruly army.

The blare of news
Insists upon its place.
Facts explode like popcorn
At the lobby refreshment stand
And we devour them
Barely chewing. We want
To know.

But what do we need to know?
That seatbelts save lives.
That toadstools should not be eaten.
That love is not just a cozy glow,
An easy operation,
Like two plus two.

Love is pain and ecstasy,
Despair and contentment

As broad as a cloudless sky.
But a father looks at a child
And what he feels
Lies beyond the reach of words,
He can only look
At the one he helped to nurture,
In his sincere but stumbling way,
And say,
I love you. I will love you always.
And in the rough and tumble of events,
This is the thing that will never change

FOREVER

How long is forever?
Longer than a minute,
Brighter than a star
In a neighboring galaxy,
Forever lingers like the hum
Of morning coffee—or tea,
If that's the preference,
Forever doesn't need a PR agent,
Or a personal trainer,
Or a long menu of useless choices.
It doesn't need to be walked,
Or taken to the emergency room
After stepping on a nail.
Forever isn't a holiday,
Arriving in a flurry of excitement,
Departing just as things are turning glum.
There's no on/off switch,
Mute button, fast forward,
Temperature control,
Fuel tank to be filled.
Forever is...well, forever.
The universe in which a vow
Is a moment so small

But so fraught that it expands
Exponentially, the words
One of the strings
That physicists speak of,
Mysterious
Unfathomable
Infinite.

CODA

Some days silent, others full of sound and...
Well, you know the rest.

Dennis Hathaway's short stories have appeared in a number of literary magazines, including TriQuarterly, the Georgia Review, and the Southwest Review, and his story collection, The Consequences of Desire, received the Flannery O'Connor Award for Short Fiction. He has worked as a journalist, building contractor, staff member of a non-profit housing corporation and YouthBuild program for at-risk youth. He lives with his wife, Laura Silagi, in Venice, California.

Laura Silagi is a native New Yorker and artist who works primarily in photography and video. She was a founding member of the feminist art group, Mother Art, and was the producer and director of the film, Mother Art Tells her Story, which has shown at a number of film festivals in the United States and Canada. With the group, The Artists Formerly Known as Women, she has exhibited installations in New York, Los Angeles, and other cities. She is currently working on a collection of her short videos.

www.ingramcontent.com/pod-product-compliance
Lightning Source LLC
Chambersburg PA
CBHW060506080526
44584CB00015B/1572